The Royal Nonesuch

Book and Cover Design by Liz Kay

ISBN: 978-0-9897837-0-5

Published by Spark Wheel Press

The Royal Nonesuch

Steven D. Schroeder

Spark Wheel Press

Omaha, NE

1.

2.

in memory of Jake Adam York

1.

THE STRAIGHT WAY WAS LOST

My best stories all start the wrong direction
on one-way streets. For more information

on parallel parking structure, try libraries.
My work turns workers to words they worry

and revert to cryptograms for *moot*
or middle-name palindromes I forgot.

I let letters to Santa and his elves
fall in postholes like burning leaves

a building, but evolving technologies
keep children abloom in my apple trees.

You could hear we're post-apocalyptic
if your ears blister in the next eclipse.

Has-been has to be my last excuse.

HAUNTED BY WATERS

Oh brother, the other shore is farther than our father
carried us across. The same current that hurries
moss and swirls of leaves leaves your ankles
broken down in rolling rocks. If you sink

to your belly for a drink, the shallows swallow.
If you try to stand and step, the deep hand reaches
your throat like alcohol. Bite like the blade
of a driftboat oar midstream and strain to change

the river's course. Fight your end of the line
how steelhead steals rod and reel. Strike
wet tinder with the pocket thunderstorm you keep

buttoned up. I rain these drops of paper on the water,
but they continue floating by you, brother.

Traveller From An Antique Land

A hogback. Another false summit.
A brother's voice in gravel and landslide.

Language of caught on the Continental
Divide, South Platte River headwaters reach

for mouths never achieved. Our mother floats
away as vapor. Our windpipes overflow
Elevenmile Reservoir with words like *slope*

but steeper. Scree-bearded, our father, who art
an artificial cliff-face gone underground so long
we forget his name or that we met him, wakes —

here in our Rocky Mountains, *wake* means valley,
sediment and travel. *Listen*, they say, *Home is range,
not coming closer. You can't prevent this ragdoll fall.*

Want To Make My Own Fuck-Ups

Your parents confirm you're the first person
to lead your best friends into the forest

and leave them following a hoofprint trail
circled forever on itself. If small enough,
children who fall from aspens drift down to dust

leafpiles golder. If you bargain with the water
demon, a diamond for your finger for your hand

in his, lean far from shore to better your pretty.
If you can find your reflection on its side,
that knife blade is safe but could cut off

half the tales you've inherited. Don't forget
a pheasant's tailfeathers will always point home.

Count on some father figure to call for you.

This Game Lends Itself To Certain Abuses

It's a simple game.

1. The ball shall be any or all of the following: plastic, foam, rubber, leather, gel, snow, stone. Sphere, spheroid, ellipsoid, cylinder, amorphous, flat. On a rope, on a tree, on fire.

1a. The ball need not be a ball or singular.

2. Do not throw the ball so high that it catches on the sky, which is just above reach if you stretch from the roof. Nor is the roof an acceptable receptacle.

3. The ball, a bat, a vampire bat, an electrified garden hose, lasers shot from outlets, a dogpile, and a peculiar feeling all may hit you again again again, raising welts and questions.

13. One player will fill up to five positions. A receiver may defend himself or, under certain circumstances, herself. The fulltime spy needs to sneak without crunching gravel or leaves.

164. Only a coward would crouch in refuge and refuse to emerge, but everyone still will, despite the taunts, until the fort-storming phase.

335. Solid or fluid, purple sugar is perfect for throwing down between rounds.

590. The score shall appear in scars on skin. A cut or a knot is worth two scrapes or three bruises.

590a. The solution for any scoring dispute is a gunfight. No arguing over who shot whom. No stealing the ball and leaving.

999.   The first team to fortillion runs wins. Otherwise, the game ends by exhaustion mercy kill, weedwhacker ambush, or guardian, but not darkness.

1000. Rules may be added or subtracted at any time or place.

1001. Don't forget to run. You always end up running somewhere.

How Do You Like Your Blueeyed Boy?

If Invisible Mr. Lift and his Amazing Bernoulli Birds
nosedived my father's balsa glider on the driveway,
where did he bury the survivors? Do I believe

in Dad despite the evidence? When I told him I feared
the darkened yard, how long before garden gnomes
started appearing in my bedroom overnight?

Sketching on plywood sheets in the garage, did he build
my character, a rogue? At the end of days exhausted
soft-tossing fastballs at my chest, did he lie

for hours, too tired to trade me for a coordinated kid?
Was I a pain until he pried me from his forehead
with my body fully grown? Why am I inside

    Dad's shadow if it's already dead?

I Chopped Down The House

Due to childhood lack of calcium schoolwide, I cannot tell a lie
without losing a tooth. The scroll saw, my buzziest shop tool, cut

classrooms into interlocking puzzle pieces. Classmates voted me
most likely to be a three-hole punch. According to Hoyle, I ruled

at dingdong ditch, my favorite way to ring my own doorbell
an anvil. My dad hid gardens worth of fertilizer inside his head,
which we also called the rumpus room. Mom remained a floor

above and sent us gnomic incantations through the vents.
My brother's boiling point skipped several centigrade levels.
To talk without static, we squickled our polydactyl cat's back
and clicked its tail into a phonejack. We turned rubble to a verb

and rubbled our vocabulary to the word *err*. Our state bird
was burgled, our state flower debt. I fled our state assessor.

Such Machinery Also Has Its Beauty

One semester each of chemistry and calculus
teaches us computers on the atomic level
become so minute no one can find their keys.

The teacher's childhood telephone, dismantled
down past cells to pass a spelling test,
reveals speakers that talk faster and faster

than sound. In that last dusty library book,
the vocation least likely to become obsolete

remains bookmaker. The gist of American history
is a device to write novels about fighting.

Literature as a homeschooled student never owns
a television. Here, learn how to engineer your own

universe with lovely gears and wires and levers.

NOTHING ELSE IN TENNESSEE

How do you get rid of a state-school grad?
Be sure to show your work for full credit.
When the screen teems with gamers demanding
a name, can you remember whether whoever died

strangled by a wrestler called Narcissus
or on the toilet? Answer *en Español*

and the form of a question. Should the bookstore
sell tornado warning sirens for 24 hours
defenestrating letters and characters
and $#@% to the gutter? Cite your sources

the Chicago way. Will you raise those fallen
grades a roommate suicide by bull's blood hazing?

For God's sake, wake up and pay for the pizza already.

I'VE HAD A PERFECTLY WONDERFUL EVENING

If by *evening* you mean *overflowing crockpot*
If by *perfectly wonderful* you mean *the same way a cage could be
        beautiful viewed from a skewed perspective*
If by *uncle* you mean *never trust a government that bugs your
        underwear with microscopic microphones*
But another *uncle* is *how did the leper cannibal die*
And one *uncle* is actually *aunt*
When you say *gather* surely it's *row the goat across the river, then
        return for the fox or the box of lettuce*
Porch is short for *ashtray*
That old standby *college* stands for *community college* and *community*
        is code for *clown* or maybe *bartending*
Take *I told you I'd bake a cake* as *I'll be back in the car for an hour*
The name *Celeste* is French for *Goddamn*
God equals *party* does not equal *partay*
If by *house* you mean *wife*
If by *again* you mean *to death* or *next month*

Imbecile, Donkey, Flax-Head, Dope, Glump, Ninny And Fool

My arms have grown too long for sharp corners,
so I cut them. I think some think *on purpose*

when *them* might not even mean *my arms.*
My best arm is a bastard sword. I fight dirty
by starting arguments about who gets
to fight first. Anybody who would try to buy

my sourcebook on remorse could *buy it.*
If I get bigger than this, I want to be a mogul,
a highrise or charisma. From the right height,

concrete can treat you softer than water.
What do they say it means when I dream
only about elevator shafts? Please oh please
may they name this disease after me.

THEIR SONS GROW SUICIDALLY

Beautiful isn't spoken aloud.

This Paxil lacks the overdose
of those backseat lovers *cold* and *cloud,*
this nude bed's not yet said screw yourself

up to stick the point of the pen

in psychiatry's eye, this dad adopts
friend nicknames that amputate the end,
this laboratory test job offers options

of food or shock from the buzzer button.

Eat that and shit and laminate
paper tattooed with blueprints and batter
your limbic system with bottles and sleep

interrupted. They call it *getting better.*

MY EQUATION FOR YOUR EXPLOSION

My brick for your break
My mother for your fucker
My finger for your cutoff

But your letters written
      so hard the neighbors heard

Your spoon bent by the force
      of blunt forehead trauma

Your *mind your own business*
      for my *own my own business*

My *has his father's eyes* reminder
      lidded under *grown up a man*

My lied again. Our tic, our tick,
our one more time. You're mine.

A Familiar Conversation

Press *1* for a conversation void
wide enough to drive a bus through,
too long to drive the distance home

with a hammer. Press *2* for a voice
based on the graveyard, for advice
longer than rusty knives. To home
in on misuse of *hone*, say *missile*

and press the issue but not the button,
or vice versa. To escalate the explosion,
say nothing. Regrettably, the last word
is *unavailable*. For *I'd better let you go*

to suggest *you'd better let me go*, press
oh, don't say *love* and stay on the line.

2.

Never Loved A Shovel

A bulldozer driver. A pirate. A pilot diving his jet above
the sun against a zeppelin. A veteran like Dad who fixes
kittens and hands out candy to kids with kittens. A cheetah

policeman with a million speeding tickets but he's still
the fastest. The guitar-est. The universe's loudest riverboat
motor inventor. Maroon or magenta or a shade of blood

not discovered yet or something. Something with stingers.
Something that changes into something else and blows up
your head if you stare too hard. Something where you make

something of yourself. Your mother. Another number
in accounting. A manajerk who would force you to work
a shift down the mine shaft even if the canary turned blue.

Appendix A. A bladejobber. Alive. A graverobber.

Don't Know Where To Start Or Where To Begin

How big did Mega Millions get? What's a buck in the funding machine? One a.m. is my lucky number.

If this is the graveyard shift, who's the robber? I'm robber, you're blue. Want to try my gluegun?

Should it be so small? That's what she said. Why think of sex or sales every six or sloppy seconds?

What are guns or butter worth? There's Mrs. Butterworth. Which is better, indicative or vindictive mood?

Do you stock inventory or stalk it? What if the customer is always left? Passive voice ain't so bad.

Have you heard the good news? Nine out of ten dentifrices bleach your teeth whiter. Whiter than what?

What can brown do for you? What's in the box? Help me help myself to Marlboros or my marbles.

Could a lost-and-found be lost? How much does one sock cost? Wholesale tailors got great taste, less filling.

Do you sell pain in cinnamon? Will you swallow a hundred proof? Prove yourself a manager.

Who puts the fun in onions? Who puts it in size of candy bars? I'm clear past Mars to the Milky Way.

What store carries ninja stars? The Army throws them in with orders.
Have you read *The Art of War*?

Ready for some football? Super Bowl Sunday is abuse-iest for retailers.
Do you still beat their deals?

Who called the cops? What starts with F and ends with iretruck? Stop,
drop, and walk off the job.

ON PAPER I'M NOT AS SCARED AS I SEEM

Geography of office wall seams defaced
by boxcutters. A box the size of Colorado
locks inside a chest the size of mine.

The data-mines free of demons except
excessive drinking. At lunch, I drink
the ink from obsolescent résumés.

Tuesday afternoon resumes its promise
of return on churn. In turns, interns
restrain and retrain me with semicolons.

A colonoscopy video will not show
how to perform your own work for cheap.
To tabulate the sheep I need to nap
on the job, I plot my bleats on graph paper.

Everything Looks Like A Target

Kid, Black Friday nighthawks dart at the red
eyes of logo, tag and security guard, slide

electronics inside lampshade containers packed
in the trash compactor, then fake a shark attack.

Some guy wants a padlock, duct tape, duffel, shovel
and lye? Never mind why when line lengths double—

tell him to try aisle nine. We must undercut
Costco casket sellers, and undercover

surveys say the ways to reach these people
are laser guidance or advertisements for raffles

they've won. If shopping-basket bombers write
our softlines off, scatter yourself as potpourri
over rows of soap and candles infused with rose.

Break My Teeth, Sir

Dear direst czar of hiring freezes, please
sup on suppli*cants*, not on suppli*cans*,
randomize your ayes and ottoman this man
under ugly Magli shoes. Why not choose

a guy who bruises easily? Who can pick
the white-collar blues on blue-collar guitar
better than you do, voodoo economic sire?
Oh throw your stipendous penny wishes, stock

and candy to stick in the cavities between
paving stones your Lexus cracks as you travel
from Commerce, Texas to Mexican sea-level
executive. Give a man a dental plan,
a root canal—Panamanian Novocain!

A Room But Empty Space

Plexiglass convention center sides and lid encase
downtown Des Moines' mid-January waste, lifesized.

One panelist flicks pennies at our feet and demands
we make ha'pennies, one picks failsafe stock winners

from the lint that lines our pockets, but both speakers
scratch and crackle because their jacks don't match

Stainmaster's matted carpet. Free for all on the expo floor,
3-D displays on how to slaughter hogs and butcher
buckshot exit wounds—only a "United"-level registration

will let us back out. The hotel elevators go to twelve
and three-fourths before cutbacks force us to climb
each other's throats. According to this brochure, we may
not state *America without fear* without fear.

GET YOUR FUCKING SHINEBOX

Chlamydia is a flower and a cash crop, so drop your pants
in a trash fire or Times Square to ensure the burning

disappears tomorrow. Ask chicks who hawk fake Prada
for some horizontal integration and try to pay

with Monopoly money. John D. Rockefeller
Plaza was the first American President, and last

was Ronald Milhous Reagan, who freed
the lunches with his concept of can

openers for tough beans. If your coffee
house needs WiFi, a broadband carrier

pigeon will fly it for a fee, but look
out for birdshit. The worst word

that you could say is *schnook.*

PIECES OF EIGHT! PIECES OF EIGHT!

Theft is property, say pirates plotting
shots and coordinates of loot at X
and why the life begins with *lie* and selfless

ends with *less*. Possession is nine-tenths
of the theft. Rebels liberate their numbers

from counterrevolutionary accounts
and count on theft as the people's opium.
Rock musicians rip off riffs and profit

sharing files from fans with air guitars,
artistars who wouldn't charge a buck

an ear to hear their licks on politics.
Money talks, bulltheft walks. Pundits call it
pirate rebel rockstar fucking cool.

What You Get For A Song

Your song sprang from hardscrabble immigrants and railway laborers
Children assembled your song for eight cents in a Hong Kong
    sweatshop
Your song shoveled out the stables daily before it broke into the
    business
The manufacturer recalled your song because its lead parts posed a
    choking hazard
Your song made better shoes and wheels and dreams and everything in
    every single size
Investors sold your song off at a profit when they ran a bustout scheme
    after the hostile takeover
How entrepreneurial your song, how transcontinental its pace, how tall
    its building
The engineers developed your song to obsolesce but not to biodegrade
Your song the benefactor funded schools on schools on schools
Only a neverending hold message supported your song
Your song lasted longer than cradle to grave
America, your song was too big to fail
Your song cost more than itself

History On The Heads Of Matches

Message written in charcoal and afloat in a bottle's throat
    Knowledge soaked in rum and ignited for insurance

Laws shrunk onto dagger blades for a game of five-finger
    Loophole cheat-sheet on a nail gambled and lost

News clipped from papers and glued to a ransom note
    Ticket printed with yesterday's date and winners

Scripture scribbled on a deposit slip and slid to the teller
    Scrip to dynamite the vault when *money* proved illegible

Map to stolen gold locked in a strongbox full of bullion
    Signs for waypoints sunk with a grapeshot leak

History who fled through marshland and hid with a hollow reed
    Story sentence run on to throw bloodhounds off the scent
        The end in a willow thicket hunters wouldn't enter

WHERE THE BANK FAILS

Lenders weigh debtors down with pounds
of Krugerrands and launder their hands
tender in the green-dyed current, see?

Back when the drowned and liquidated
had it gooood, hoo boy, a dime could buy

a dollar and dry land. Those who forget
the past are destined to—what's the rest?—

oh yes, be swindled of their PINs, investments
and fins. Our founders bank, spend,

founder and sink in squander. Benjamin get
your bindle from despond, swim the English

language and switch the channel to celebrity
double entendres on the bubble bubble.

TIME IS MONEY

Many, many times is regulations.

Money doesn't float. Wet concrete
is faster than a contract signature.

Track tax deadlines in the distance
from red X-marks on homework
to five-bar gates for prison time.

Laundry has the same given name
as money. On this loan agreement,
interest rates exceed your weight
in waiting rooms and DMV lines

times your lifespan. Money claims
you can understand the numbers
if only you work hard enough.

No Owners, Only Spenders

Cash makes you fun. A check can stop
without your help and when it wants.
Credit cards only hurt themselves.

The way to Valhalla is open
your wallet. For a goldmine, open

a vein. Oh platinum account,
how else could two months' salary
buy some more time? We should replace

your girlfriends since our company
is people too. If you would choose
never to sleep with us, remember

please dream American. To save
your country, pay until you're spent.

POOR, TO USE A VULGAR EXPRESSION

Poverty is not a genetic trait but a lifestyle choice
    Not about slavery but states' rights and taxation
        Not a crime of desire but of power and control

Poverty is ten times likelier at home than in the workplace
    The leading cause of schoolyard insult rhymes worldwide
        Popular among key demographics advertisers covet

A more tasteful term for poverty might be collateral damage
    Revenue adjustment on the highway to economic hope
        Society's last penny put down on the railroad track

Coins dropped off skyscrapers fall fast enough to kill poverty
    Coins stacked high as skyscrapers could pay for poverty
        All coins in the United States contain traces of poverty
        The next coin flip is due to come up prosperity

3.

Each One Goes Alone

Late-night regret comes on as a brunette
is a bullshit line yet felt right at the time.

When you pick a new city for foliage and brick
in promotional photos, the baggage follows.
Of course, the *you* is *me* who packs the freight

hidden so long in the attic behind a metaphor
that handwritten notes under the door don't say
so long but split into letters, forget the distance
from *disassemble* to *dissemble* and the message

this might misstate that it works better if you try
not to talk about what makes it work. After a break

on whatever levels of the word, we can make up
reasons to repeat these moves we make, Love.

You Won't Find A New Land

Colorado   are we do-over or overdue
Oh   Colorado   did you send my *737* a centennial tailwind
And   Colorado   can we define two kinds of abandon on the Kansas
    border
Do you remember Denver   Colorado   all night counting train cars
    through the starlit screen
Those days I couldn't hold your microbrews   Colorado   didn't I say
    you bewitch
Colorado   were you the I in blizzard and was I snowblind eyes with
    both of us this close to closure
Is your state state moving   Colorado   and what way   Colorado
Does your name   Colorado   truly mean *family responsibilities* in
    Spanish
When I recombine your letters   Colorado   why don't I see you in them
    anymore
And why are your lines so long   Colorado   since this longing is longer
How far corner to corner   Colorado   before we declare *no más*
Where to place your accent   Colorado   when you have none
If I call you   Colorado   will you   call me home?

FLUTTER FODDER

Hummingbird fights over sugarwater overheat.
Almendrado, amaretto, sweet-and-sour, Sprite, lime,
and palpitate it as the drumbeat in "La Grange"
sweats out pounds. Astride the straight and narrow

divider between *arrest* and *rest*, nightfall counts
down to eighty degrees in threes, speed enforced
by air conditioner. Mosquito-bite burglaries
recirculate blood and bloody currency citywide
fast as a pokeweed sprout grows fat, but barely

firefly enough to blow the nozzle off a bottle
rocket. Somewhere, summer fits in an icechest
the volume of a fist duet. June first is the letter
roar unread, a murmur later after English ends.

A Place To Hang Your Head

Unfinished as the basement, nightfall
drip-drips from pipe fittings and creeps
in non-egress windows — no bars means no

burglary yet. Two doors require three keys,
but one freezes in ghettobird floodlight.
Deadbolt your bedroom to keep out

sleep and break-ins by kin who chatter
at your attic squirrels. Yes, that's our pickup
idling outside, no we will not help you

move again, and no you're not invited
to our party and/or fight. The last owner left

through default and walls made of holes.
That hallway leads to nobody.

Face Like a Barndoor

Yours is a fastfood milkshake, exactly
the same shape as a cold shoulder of beef.

Mine they serve all night at Waffle House,
smothered and covered by the waitress.

Oh my last salt-shriveled fry, the menu
pictures never match our actuality.

The cook couldn't use each pound of cow
in our countenances, so he hid its hide
and sun-dried heart under our bed.

Let us return our shit sandwich openfaced
to the farmyard. Let us tomato onions
at old McDonald's salmonella. And let us,
driving through, stop to pet the piglets.

WHAT MOVES IN THE ATTIC

In their apartment? Below, we believe
we know — *thud* of yanked off the bed
by the ankles. There lies another story split

leveled above. Their eyes diagonal over eggs
over easy, uneasy over groaning hardwood
gaps in the timeline, allnight signs dark, dark

darker in their hair. *Thud thud* of hearts in each
other's mouths. Here, noise complaints from us
no use against the arguments of alcohol

or onomatopoeia of murmur, gasp and sigh
past four a.m., unaware of underfloors.
How can we have ourselves shut up there?

Thud thud thud on our downstairs door.

Uncertain Stumbling Buzz

It's slurtainly curtain time to head for bed —
        mattress, back seat or wastebasket
      matter the same, a semi-stranger, number
        dialed to learn if it's too late
to call, old stories retold, incomplete
sentences, blanks full of what
     words a drink thunks up.
        Stomach sprawled downstairs,
dollars dropped on cards, and piss on alley walls
     all fall only on days that end
    in *day*. If dazes that follow hold more
bars and ways to lose an eye or four, they must
        be fun. This car sure stunny fumbles.

NOBODY WITH A GOOD CAR

Arrives late for a party or turns down
bootlegger reverses to elude the *Federales*,

inverts *Pergo* for *pergola* or burns the host
of code phrases learned from the German gentleman.

Answer *The covenants state that white is not an earthtone*
with *Butterfly knife is no kind of lifestyle.*

This is an escargot fork—left tine goes in light sockets,
right in a henchman's eyeball. Unseen, a ninja
can punch through your ribcage and show you

ninety-nine ways to fill a cheese-platter
if you fail to explain or raise his latest credit score.

For safety's sake, maybe we could take separate cars,
you the Honda and I the Hyundai.

LOVERS WHO CAN'T QUITE WORK IT

Knock once and I'm coming down with some sinusy thing.
Knock twice and it's two too many for me to notice.
Knock four without three first and you can submit
your proposal letter in sextuplicate through the mail slot.

Push this button too far for the budget bedroom tour.
Push this button of mine to indicate whose and who's remote.
Push this button downstairs from the second story
you tell about how you went garden to garage to garbage.

Leave a message at the tone the tone of voice you use
leaves no doubt I'm right to let you hear and let me hear it.
Leave your love by the sliver of livingroom window I left
open just enough to screen your gift of a single lavender leaf.
Leave me alone if you want to see this "us" alive again.

CODE NAME IS THE ONLY ONE

When I say *the chicken hawk sleeps alone*
isn't much of an introduction, it's not
like I can finish a round of Double Agent

without a hangover. The names and ranks
I do not have to be tortured to give up
of individuals whose lives I do not envy
may be disinformation for celebrity patrons

I fabulize. The game where one of us plays
the spy is too easy if there's just one of us.
The password is *passive-aggressive*.
After you crack, is my cover whatever?

Why can't you guess this picture I encrypted
in invisible ink? It's obvious it's loneliness.

ANOTHER WORD THAT RHYMES WITH SHAME

The same damn word that rhymes with *got no rhythm*   but not with
   not to blame
That spells *embarrassed* for some parlor game   but can't recall how
   many r's there are
The word that synthesizes every sin in whiskey on the rocks   but
   makes it double
That fills whole Hawthorne novels never read   but bluffed and called
   in conversation
Defines the introvert who wants to ghost from small talk   but whose
   lurch says ghoul

Yet spoken upside-down and backward   casts a cantrip that can turn
   left right
Becomes an anagram for *hit the shot*   and *blindfolded through
   pinhole hoops of flame*
An artifice that builds a shield from a bullet   and befriends the gun
   that sent it
A code to tell pit traps from treasures on unlettered maps   and to
   unlock the crypt
The single word that means a flock of blackbirds   and the means to
   sing their flight

Yet still this answer for the stolen riddle story ends   in silence,
   awkward silence
Shorthand for wired-reflex card-mechanic prestidigitation   bested by
   stick-finger irony
A foolproof mnemonic hook for your true name   but mispronounced
   again   *you fool, you fool*

Something Might Be Gaining On You

That's not my name, I told the neighbors
when I fell and they found me calling
Happy, that's my Doxie mix,
gone up sixteen years this Sunday.

Are you my son? If so, which one?
No, I named mine James and Jacob

and James, the oldest, who stole my mail
except the bills, so we're not speaking.
Though Doctor Blake made me promise
to take those pills, I flushed them because

he's a black. I looked back but couldn't see
the voice who whispered *Hello, Crazy Lee.*

Anyway, that's not my name.

Might As Well Live

If you knew you could hear this, you might have
thrown yourself under the bus. Too soon?

Someone said someone ought to say a few words
unlike *knuckle* and *blackjack* and *smoke*,

So we offered our testimonies to the best
of your recollection, which pled the fifth
that hid behind the Pledge and Drano bottles.

In our version, your heart wasn't on a milk carton,
you were the bad news bad news got, you saw
a doctor because your eyes chose good over evil.

When we closed your eyes for good, you looked
like you were checking the lids for pinpricks.

When we closed ours, we could deny everything.

I Do Not Think It Means What You Think It Means

Can you find a thesaurus listing for us?
    Our synonyms for rumor are all but one untrue.
        Friends of friends forward the word they hear.

Do you find my dishevelry tragic or attractive?
    I am certainly the most invertebrate of flirts.
        Our relationship status is unattainable.

Do I only do what I do do with you with you?
    Add *in bed* after any of my statements (in bed).
        We're Pete and Repeat sitting in a boat.

If I complement you, will you compliment me?
    When I'm with you, don't whisper implications.
        When I'm incognito, tell everyone I'm cute.
           When I'm gone, say I was beautiful.

4.

STRIKING THIRTEEN

We the [Expletive Deleted] of the [Classified Data]
    Undefeated when the blame game goes sudden death
        Under goddamn the torpedoes and transparencies

In order that over half not understand they mean *majority*
    Under orders to drown the word *public* in the town fountain
        In order from most to most important contract awards

Choose a czar for the war on war on military metaphor
    Whose strikes are surgical and whose fire is live
        Depending on your meanings of *choice* and *life*

Like the energy defense industry's business is yours
    If the definition of *is* isn't *is* but *isn't* or if *yours* is *ours*

(Please refer to the Child Protection Act footnotes
    Subhead *You Must Have Missed That Meeting*)

TROUBLE THERE ON THE FRONTIER

When water and government and children disappear
we take apocalyptic scripture seriouser and seriouser.

Coyotes mentor hens in history of the West they alter,
chant *chicken neck chicken foot* then put them on the altar.

Legs of rumor running down this cowtown spread
plagues and fantail sprays colored chorus-girl red.

Hot shotgun hut admits no sunlight so we burn it.
Horse of course can't recanter its curses so we burn it.

We draw Colt Peacemakers and X's all over our maps
traveled in covered wagons circling back to traps.

Autocracy and automobile and automatic buffalo
sheriff's deputies and dentists moved from Buffalo.
Trainhorn, don't you know there's no return to buffalo?

No Hope Except In Arms

This knife sells itself
This assault rifle will change your life
This rocket launcher is a limited-time offer
This hand grenade can shred a head of lettuce in under seven seconds
    guaranteed, or we'll refund your money
This armor-piercing bullet kills 99 percent of household fungi, molds
    and mildews
This autocannon disinfects the world's surface for our descendants
This fighter jet is part of a complete breakfast
This aircraft carrier cares
This main battle tank thanks the good Lord and its mama
This cruise missile redefines its mission so it never misses school plays
This bunker-buster bomb is user friendly, idiot proof and child safe for
    the entire family to enjoy, eight to 88
This gun wants to tuck your kids into bed
This one would fuck anybody

Up Up Down Down Left Right Left Right B A Start

You have infinity lives plus one. Walk through
that wall headfirst without collision. Walk through

a million mall-store backgrounds backward to steal
money without a gun. If you trip into a jail cell,

Drop your name out the keyhole, and the sentry
will release it. If you stop time for a century

to skip a puzzle, pause two to maximize
your dexterity and explosive abilities

by balancing sixteen sticks of dynamite.
To restore your health when hurt, devour meat

or type the curse of *QWERTY* right-to-left.
To escape the loop of the world on cheat, reset

yourself in safe. You now have no life left.

Only The Name Of The Airport Changes

For your safety the maximum magazine size is now
lifesaver or however many metric ounces in a dozen

inches of vigilance, no questions please, you must
opt out of your "accidental" bathroom-camera mugshot
via fax or Pony Express of a safety-word waiver request

maze unsolvable except with a feather pen whose chicken
doesn't fly but plucks toothpicks and suspicious facial
moisturizers from some orifice, our stun-gun safety is on

the honor system that officers respond within six weeks
if you dismember your unclearance number Q-Safe-T,
here's a hoop through which you have the right to jump

the line when you pay a patriot convenience fee, but once
we play the safety card you'd better pray for cancellation.

NOTHING HAS EVER HAPPENED, AND NOTHING EVER WILL

Coming up, find out about a common home appliance
    that causes short-term memory loss, and tomorrow
        an appliance that causes short-term memory loss

Chet lets us know what weather beast with whetted teeth
    will chew through both your femurs this weekend

Learn from a spokesperson whether police believe
    dozens of prison escapees live on your block
        or a country farm where they can run and run

We'll tell who or whom we spied hiding in your closet
    tonight, but deny the idea we might have been behind
        door #2 instead of outside your bedroom window

And why do you store rat poison under the counter
    for your toddler Jennifer to find? Stay tuned.

ONE FRAME FAMOUS

Everything is falling up or sideways,
everybody breathless as a windstorm

walls the water solid. Someone's body
hits a river branch and breaks in half.

Someone else's, fast as avalanches
crystallizing, hits at least a hundred

miles per hour. Someone's fingertip hits
buttons, and his voice replaces sirens

with descriptions of them. Chyrons rattle
death-rate stats for boats in flames. Volcano,

C-break, tidal wave, tornado, C-break,
earthquake. Dry, unseen offscreen, the anchor

asks again *What country is this in?*

BETTER CONSIDER MY NATIONAL RESOURCES

Oh say can you see my cheese fries, my display of potato chips shaped
　　like states, my hot-dog-eating contest, my Colonel's secret recipe,
　　my finger-licking, my stuffing
God shed his grace on my have you heard the good news, my eyes have
　　seen the glory, my shotgun chapel neon off the Las Vegas strip, my
　　stolen Gideon bible with lines crossed out, my God
I pledge allegiance to my highball Jack and Coke, my tobacco leaf, my
　　meth-mouth tooth decay, my crack-baby exorcism, my high on
　　life, my ditch behind the high school
I only regret that I have but one life to give for my third job at
　　7-Eleven, my automotive manufacturer bought at auction for
　　a nickel, my drive-in movie, my drive-through liquor store, my
　　drive-by
Give me liberty or give me my Brink's armored car, my Pinkertons on
　　every corner, my unmarked and non-sequential twenty-dollar bills,
　　my vault door opened to reveal nothing
The only thing we have to fear is my pinup, my prenup, my pushed her
　　in where she would drown, my poured-concrete Supermax cell,
　　my lay down the law, my lay, my lie
Be all you can be in my pants, my is that a pistol in your pocket, my
　　that's what she said, my Omaha hi-lo poker if you know what I
　　mean, my O-face, my oh my
A house divided against itself cannot stand my capital of Idaho is
　　I, my I dunno, my sabermetric statistics versus my guesstimate,
　　my underwater nest of cottonmouths, my urban myth
Speak softly and carry my billy club, my bully pulpit, my pit bull on a
　　chain, my smoke billows bellowing lungs out, my sniper's ghillie
　　suit, my fully poseable Snake Eyes action figure

We hold these truths to be my exclusion for pre-existing conditions, my
    odds of winning one in 6.4 million, my four to six weeks for
    delivery, my don't try this at home, my rights reserved
We shall overcome my Fighting Irish, my *donde esta el baño*, my
    Columbus Day parade, my swing low sweet chariot, my Defense
    of Marriage Act, my miscegenation, my nation
Don't fire until you see the whites of my Black Friday, my Downy
    dryer sheets, my letters to Haiti, my vanity license plate H8E, my
    way or the highway, my credit card declined by the ATM
Don't tread on my Deadwood, my marshal with a Stetson hat, my
    desperado with a Mexican necktie, my this land is my land, my
    mine, my mine, my mine

Buried Among Those Mountains

You wake in a box. You unlock the box. You take the box.
North is inertia, south not nothing, west rejection, east unrest.
You spin to dizziness and guess. You take the easiest digression.

Back is the new black, left is back, right is wrong, forward you rue.
Outside the box is think. Inside are cyanide and innuendo.
You take advice and medicine. You drink a suicide of information.

After you is paranoia, before forlorn, follow is gossip, lead is lost.
You take no chance. You randomize your choices with dice.
Through the box is truth. Overcome is them but never you.

You take a curve. You turn into a driveway. You race into a house.
Around the box are climb and fall. Surrounded is fall asleep again.
Up is taken, down cliché, and inclined is a terrible thing to waste.
You find mountains impassible in all directions. You select *impossible*.

OF THE DEVIL'S PARTY

We synergized lollipops and roller coasters.
We own a rockin' van. You want to get in

hot gates? You're on the list. You want to lay
hands on the baby goats? They're fake but bait
foxes out of foxholes for us to lionize.

You want to save your friends from drowning
if they bob forbidden apples? Have a map
for the revival scavenger hunt. You want a hint?

Chant *Daredevil Evel Knievel revs in heaven*
seven times, gun the engine and huff the fumes.

You want fun? Just sign your name and drop
your keys in the slot. Can't stop, or you go home
lonesome and hopeless. We don't want that, do we?

Gin Don't Mess With Me

Beefeater confabulates better drivers. Over half
of Americans believe the Soviet government

invented vodka to subsidize potato bugs and juice
baby bottles. They're right. No matter what you hear,

the world's largest prairie dog carries no plague fleas.
These knees forecast storms. Over half of Americans
not of Mexican descent know the Mayan calendar

portends Armageddon in four, plus or minus three.
In craps, the optimum time to bet the pass line is two,
the object to rig one new pair of shoes and sock it
away for the house. Over half of Americans owe

more green than they mow and water their lawns.
Even sinners mustn't mess with gin. Amen.

A Pontificating Bird

The red-tailed hawk's claws tore
the bunny up. Big Bird perched
on Schoolhouse Rock and plucked
Bugs Bunny with his *B* is for *beak*.

The head-tailed roc duckstrum
the wordbotcher. The hack parched
on Iraq and misundevoured
the bungle. You unhooded the hawk

and skinned the bunny, or
you hawked the bunny, ducked

and swallowed. Defeat and declaw
tore up deduct before devour.

Murder your little birdies.

EPILOGUE FOR MONSTERS

Hush little baby, don't you pry: Chicken Little
lets the crib fall, Little Boy Blue always wins
on black but blows it rolling snake eyes.

Yes, all still small. If the itsy bitsy spider
grifts ants in gutters and Red Riding Hood cries
neither *what big teeth* nor *wolf* but *uncle*,

does it matter, oh you who needs to know
too much? One monkey joins a magic show
and splits in two bananas. These piggies split

the opposite of slops before their owners go
broke to sleep and wake up at the bacon auction.

Half of every storyteller cuts the other off —
some say *shit* a lot, some shut their mouths.

THEY JUST GAVE ME THE NUMBER WHEN I WAS YOUNG

Thirteen rolled on loaded dice for luck
    Thirteen heart tattoos in red and black
        Thirteen nooses not enough to hang

Thirteen leaps across the Colorado
    Thirteen talents bottomless in pockets
        Thirteen days concocting fireproof jackets
           Thirteen nights asleep in a tornado

Thirteen grown coyotes fought and pinned
    Thirteen scars from fourteen different battles
        Thirteen doorways barred by trickster riddles
          Thirteen rattlesnakes as a hatband

Thirteen lives revived by age thirteen
    Thirteen lies believed by line thirteen

TRANSGRESSIONS

Acknowledgements

Thank you to Aaron Anstett, Sandra Beasley, Eduardo C. Corral, Oliver de la Paz, John Gallaher, David Keplinger, Dora Malech, Adrian Matejka, Richard Newman, Erika L. Sánchez, and Jake Adam York. Thank you to Liz Kay, Jen Lambert, and Spark Wheel Press.

Previous publications (probably in different form):

1913: A Journal of Forms – "Break My Teeth, Sir," "Don't Know Where to Start or Where to Begin," & "Get Your Fucking Shinebox"
The Bakery – "Might as Well Live"
Barn Owl Review – "Want to Make My Own Fuck-Ups"
Cimarron Review – "A Room but Empty Space"
The Collagist – "Everything Looks like a Target"
Copper Nickel – "I Chopped Down the House"
Country Dog Review – "My Equation for Your Explosion"
Country Music – "Lovers Who Can't Quite Work It," "Nobody with a Good Car," "Striking Thirteen," & "Where the Bank Fails"
Court Green – "Never Loved a Shovel"
Diode – "Haunted By Waters" & "What Moves in the Attic"
Drunken Boat – "Only the Name of the Airport Changes"
Fourteen Hills – "No Hope Except in Arms"
Front Porch – "Nothing Else in Tennessee" & "Pieces of Eight! Pieces of Eight!"
Hot Metal Bridge – "Better Consider My National Resources"
Indiana Review – "Up Up Down Down Left Right Left Right B A Start"
InDigest – "Each One Goes Alone," "Such Machinery Also Has Its Beauty," & "Time Is Money"
Jet Fuel Review – "Another Word That Rhymes with Shame"

The Journal – "Face like a Barndoor" & "I've Had a Perfectly Wonderful Evening"

The Laurel Review – "I Do Not Think It Means What You Think It Means," "Of the Devil's Party," & "On Paper I'm Not as Scared as I Seem"

The Nepotist – "Something Might Be Gaining on You"

New England Review – "How Do You Like Your Blueeyed Boy" & "Uncertain Stumbling Buzz"

The Offending Adam – "Gin Don't Mess with Me"

Pebble Lake Review – "No Owners, Only Spenders" & "One Frame Famous"

Pleiades – "Trouble There on the Frontier"

Prime Number – "Imbecile, Donkey, Flax-Head, Dope, Glump, Ninny and Fool" & "A Place to Hang Your Head"

Sawbuck – "They Just Gave Me the Number When I Was Young"

Sou'wester – "The Straight Way Was Lost"

South Dakota Review – "Buried Among Those Mountains," "Flutter Fodder," & "You Won't Find a New Land"

The Southeast Review – "This Game Lends Itself to Certain Abuses"

Sugar House Review – "Traveller from an Antique Land"

Thrush Poetry Journal – "Code Name Is the Only One," "Nothing Has Happened, and Nothing Ever Will," & "What You Get for a Song"

The UCity Review – "A Pontificating Bird," "History on the Heads of Matches," & "Poor, to Use a Vulgar Expression"

Waccamaw – "A Familiar Conversation"

Washington Square – "Epilogue for Monsters"

Whiskey Island – "Their Sons Grow Suicidally"

NOTES

Where I stole the titles:
"Another Word That Rhymes with Shame" – Nirvana, "Blew"
"Better Consider My National Resources" – Allen Ginsberg, "America"
"Break My Teeth, Sir" – Olena Kalytiak Davis, "Six Apologies, Lord"
"Buried Among Those Mountains" – Geronimo
"Code Name Is the Only One" – The Roots, "The Seed (2.0)"
"Don't Know Where to Start or Where to Begin" – Patton Oswalt
"Each One Goes Alone" – Ursula Le Guin, "The Ones Who Walk
    Away from Omelas"
"Epilogue for Monsters" – Roberto Bolaño, *Nazi Literature in the
    Americas*
"Everything Looks like a Target" – Clutch, "Binge and Purge"
"Face like a Barndoor" – Robert Creeley, "A Wicker Basket"
"A Familiar Conversation" – Aesop, "The Fox and the Lion"
"Flutter Fodder" – Dora Malech, "Remains"
"Get Your Fucking Shinebox" – *Goodfellas*
"Gin Don't Mess with Me" – Harryette Mullen, *Muse & Drudge*
"Haunted by Waters" – Norman Maclean, *A River Runs Through It*
"History on the Heads of Matches" – Jake Adam York, "Secession"
"How Do You Like Your Blueeyed Boy?" – E. E. Cummings, "Buffalo
    Bill's"
"I Chopped Down the House" – Kenneth Koch, "Variations on a
    Theme by William Carlos Williams"
"I Do Not Think It Means What You Think It Means" – William
    Goldman, *The Princess Bride*
"I've Had a Perfectly Wonderful Evening" – Groucho Marx
    (apocryphal)
"Imbecile, Donkey, Flax-Head, Dope, Glump, Ninny and Fool" – Isaac
    Bashevis Singer, "Gimpel the Fool"

"Lovers Who Can't Quite Work It" – Mary Biddinger, "Snakeskin"

"Might as Well Live" – Dorothy Parker, "Résumé"

"My Equation for Your Explosion" – Sandra Beasley, "My Los Alamos"

"Never Loved a Shovel" – The Clash, "Bankrobber"

"No Hope Except in Arms" – Niccolò Machiavelli, *The Prince*

"No Owners, Only Spenders" – *The Wire*

"Nobody with a Good Car" – Flannery O'Connor, *Wise Blood*

"Nothing Else in Tennessee" – Wallace Stevens, "Anecdote of the Jar"

"Nothing Has Ever Happened, and Nothing Ever Will" – Gabriel García Márquez, *One Hundred Years of Solitude*

"Of the Devil's Party" – William Blake, *The Book of Heaven and Hell*

"On Paper I'm Not as Scared as I Seem" – Clay Matthews, "A Pilgrim's Progress, or Lack Thereof"

"One Frame Famous" – Aaron Anstett, "Prayer Against Dying on Camera"

"Only the Name of the Airport Changes" – Italo Calvino, *Invisible Cities*

"Pieces of Eight! Pieces of Eight!" – Robert Louis Stevenson, *Treasure Island*

"A Place to Hang Your Head" – Warren Zevon, "Things to Do in Denver When You're Dead"

"A Pontificating Bird" – *The Merriam-Webster Encyclopedia of Literature*

"Poor, to Use a Vulgar Expression" – Thomas Malthus, *An Essay on the Principle of Population*

"A Room but Empty Space" – Laozi, *Tao Te Ching*

The Royal Nonesuch – Mark Twain, *The Adventures of Huckleberry Finn*

"Something Might Be Gaining on You" – Satchel Paige

"The Straight Way Was Lost" – Dante Alighieri, *Inferno*

"Striking Thirteen" – George Orwell, *1984*

"Such Machinery Also Has Its Beauty" – Marie Curie

"Their Sons Grow Suicidally" – James Wright, "Autumn Begins in Martins Ferry, Ohio"

"They Just Gave Me the Number When I Was Young" – Johnny Cash, "Thirteen"

"This Game Lends Itself to Certain Abuses" – Bill Watterson, *Calvin and Hobbes*

"Time Is Money" – Benjamin Franklin, "Advice to a Young Tradesman"

"Traveller from an Antique Land" – Percy Shelley, "Ozymandias"

"Trouble There on the Frontier" – Timothy Liu, "Westward"

"Uncertain Stumbling Buzz" – Emily Dickinson, "(465) I Heard a Fly Buzz"

"Up Up Down Down Left Right Left Right B A Start" – The Konami code, *Contra*

"Want to Make My Own Fuck-Ups" – PJ Harvey, "The Pocket Knife"

"What Moves in the Attic" – Gina Franco, *Utter*

"What You Get for a Song" – Alexander Solzhenitsyn, *One Day in the Life of Ivan Denisovich*

"Where the Bank Fails" – John Gallaher, "American Rivers"

"You Won't Find a New Land" – Constantine Cavafy, "The City"

Steven D. Schroeder's first book was *Torched Verse Ends* (BlazeVOX [books], 2009). His poetry is available from *New England Review, Pleiades, Verse, The Journal, Indiana Review, Barrow Street,* and *Verse Daily.* Poems have also appeared by invitation in city parks, public transportation, and business waiting rooms. He edits the online poetry journal *Anti-,* serves as co-curator for Observable Readings, and works as a Certified Professional Résumé Writer. Long a resident of Colorado, he now lives in St. Louis.

www.ingramcontent.com/pod-product-compliance
Lightning Source LLC
Chambersburg PA
CBHW051736040426
42447CB00008B/1161